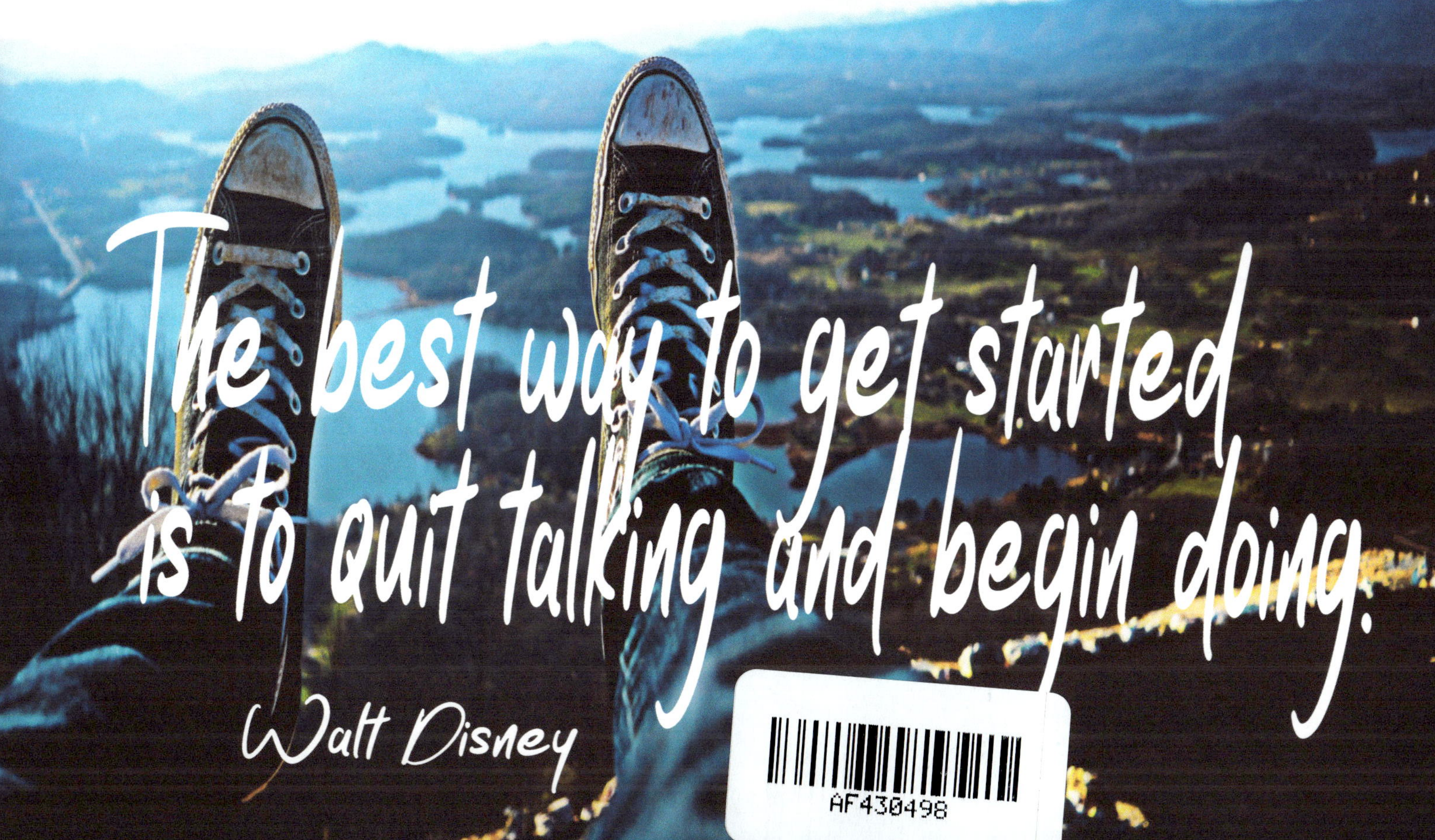

The best way to get started is to quit talking and begin doing.
Walt Disney
AF430498

The pessimist sees difficulty in every opportunity. The optimist sees opportunity in every difficulty.
Winston Churchill

JAN / 2021

S	M	T	W	T	F	S
					New Year's Day 1	2
3	4	5	6	7	8	9
10	11	12	13	14	15	16
17	Martin Luther King Jr 18	19	20	21	22	23
24	25	26	27	28	29	30
31						

Don't let yesterday take up
too much of today.

Will Rogers

FEB / 2021

S M T W T F S
1 2 3 4 5 6
7 8 9 10 11 12 13
14 Presidents' Day 15 16 17 18 19 20
21 22 23 24 25 26 27
28

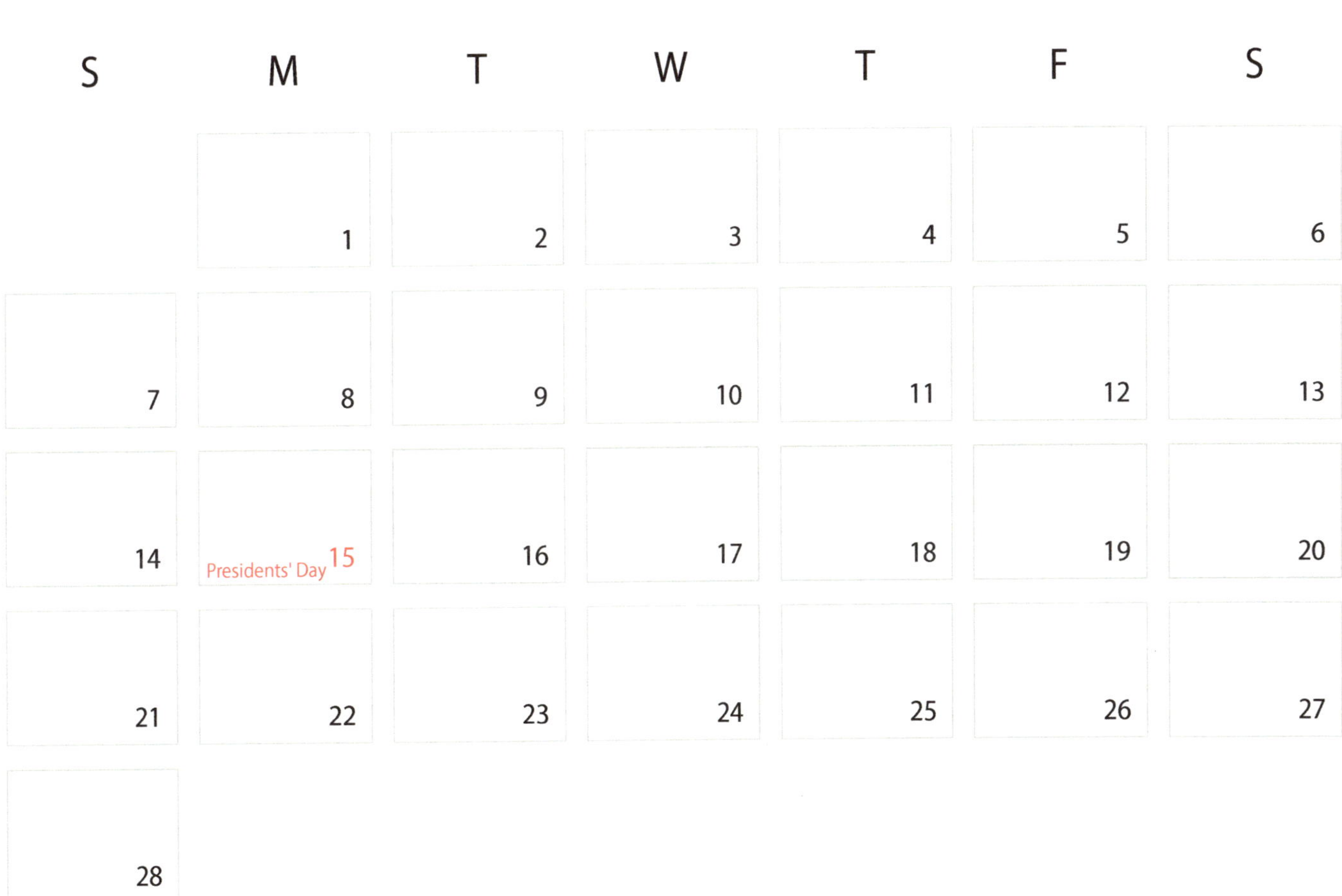

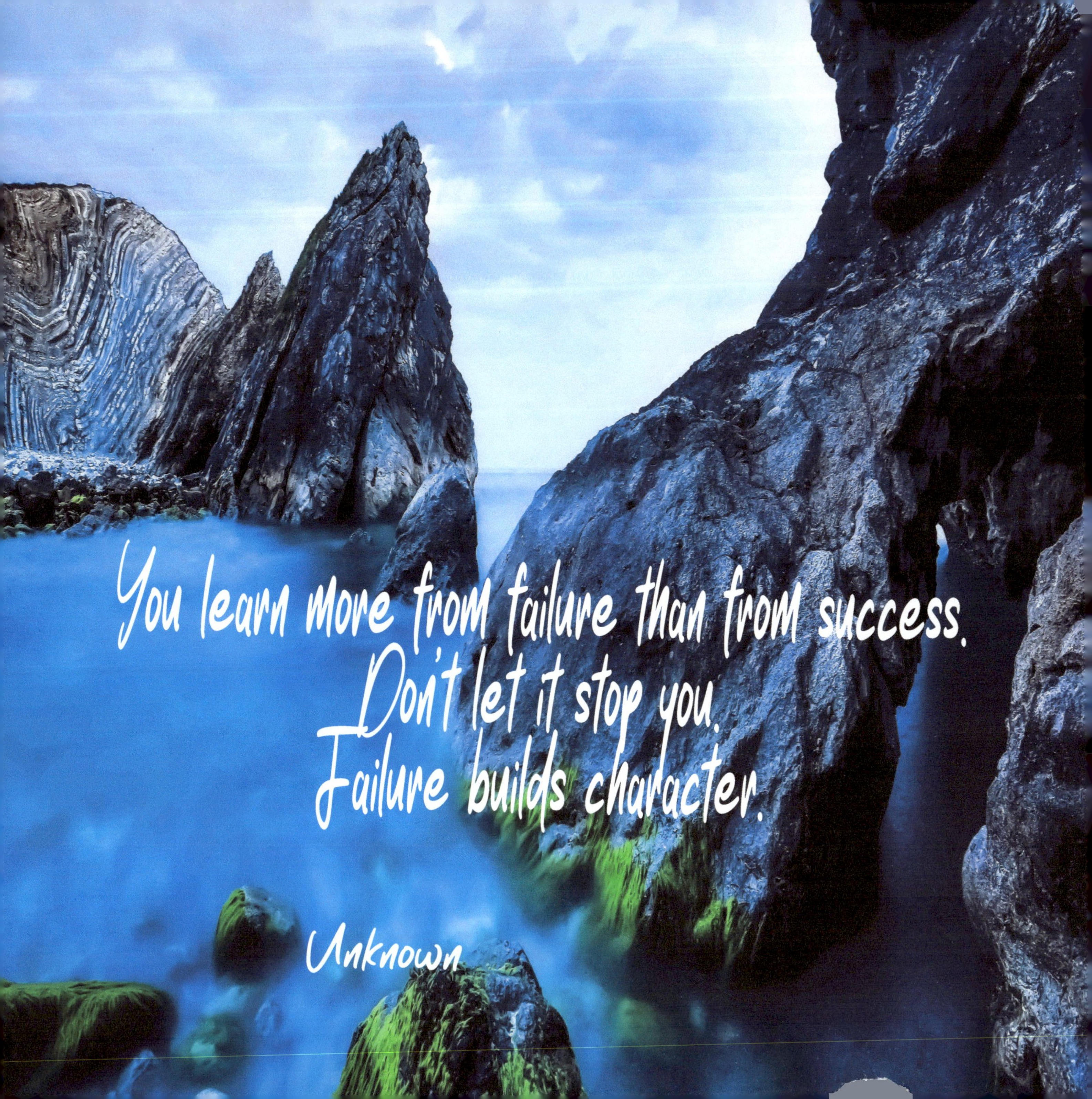
You learn more from failure than from success.
Don't let it stop you.
Failure builds character.

Unknown

MAR / 2021

S	M	T	W	T	F	S
	1	2	3	4	5	6
7	8	9	10	11	12	13
14	15	16	17	18	19	20
21	22	23	24	25	26	27
28	29	30	31			

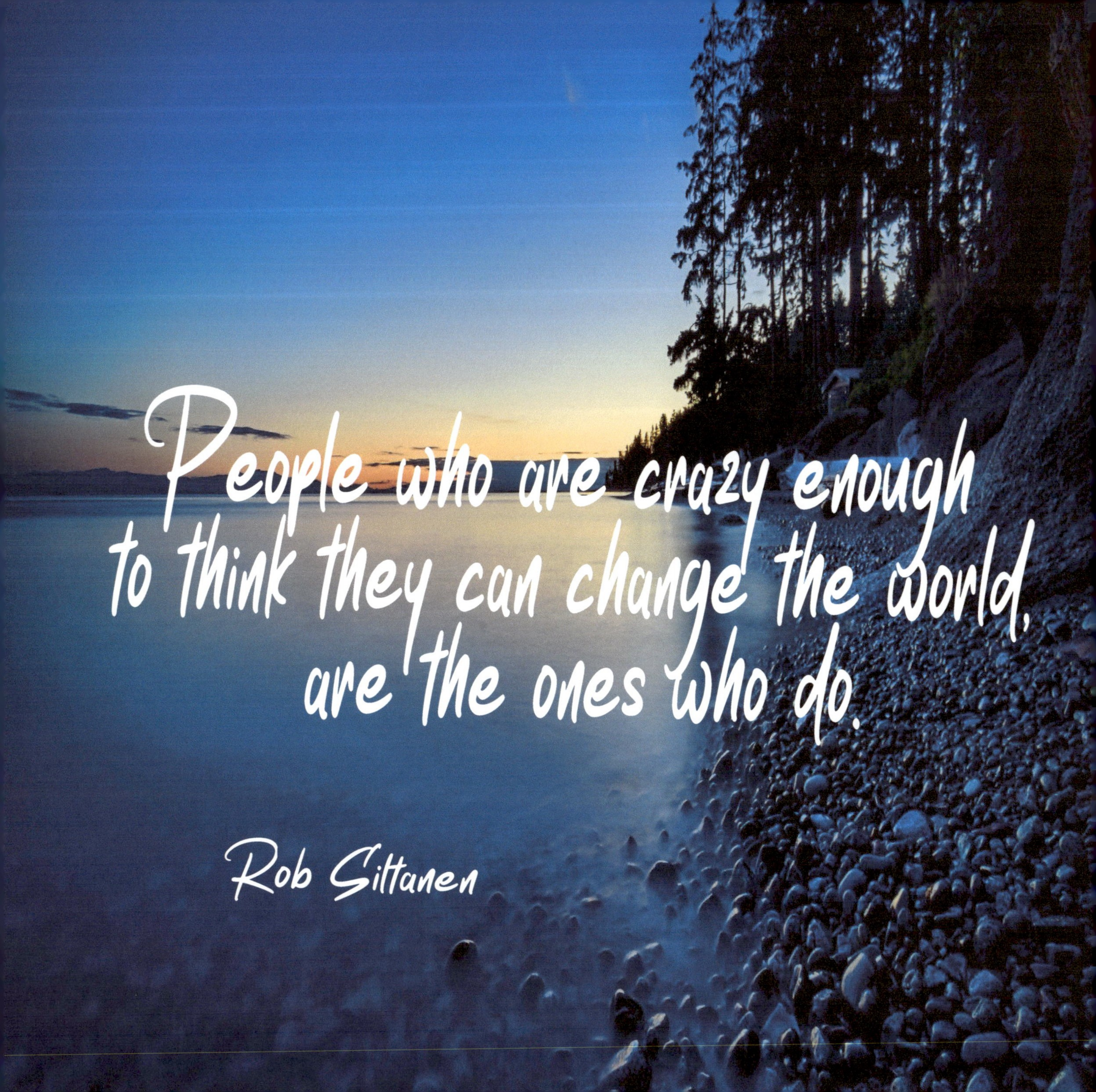

People who are crazy enough
to think they can change the world,
are the ones who do.

Rob Siltanen

APR / 2021

S	M	T	W	T	F	S
				1	2	3
4	5	6	7	8	9	10
11	12	13	14	15	16	17
18	19	20	21	22	23	24
25	26	27	28	29	30	

If you are working on something that you really care about, you don't have to be pushed.

Steve Jobs

MAY / 2021

S	M	T	W	T	F	S
						1
2	3	4	5	6	7	8
9	10	11	12	13	14	15
16	17	18	19	20	21	22
23	24	25	26	27	28	29
30	Memorial Day 31					

It's not whether you get knocked down, its whether you get up.

JUN / 2021

S	M	T	W	T	F	S
		1	2	3	4	5
6	7	8	9	10	11	12
13	14	15	16	17	18	19
20	21	22	23	24	25	26
27	28	29	30			

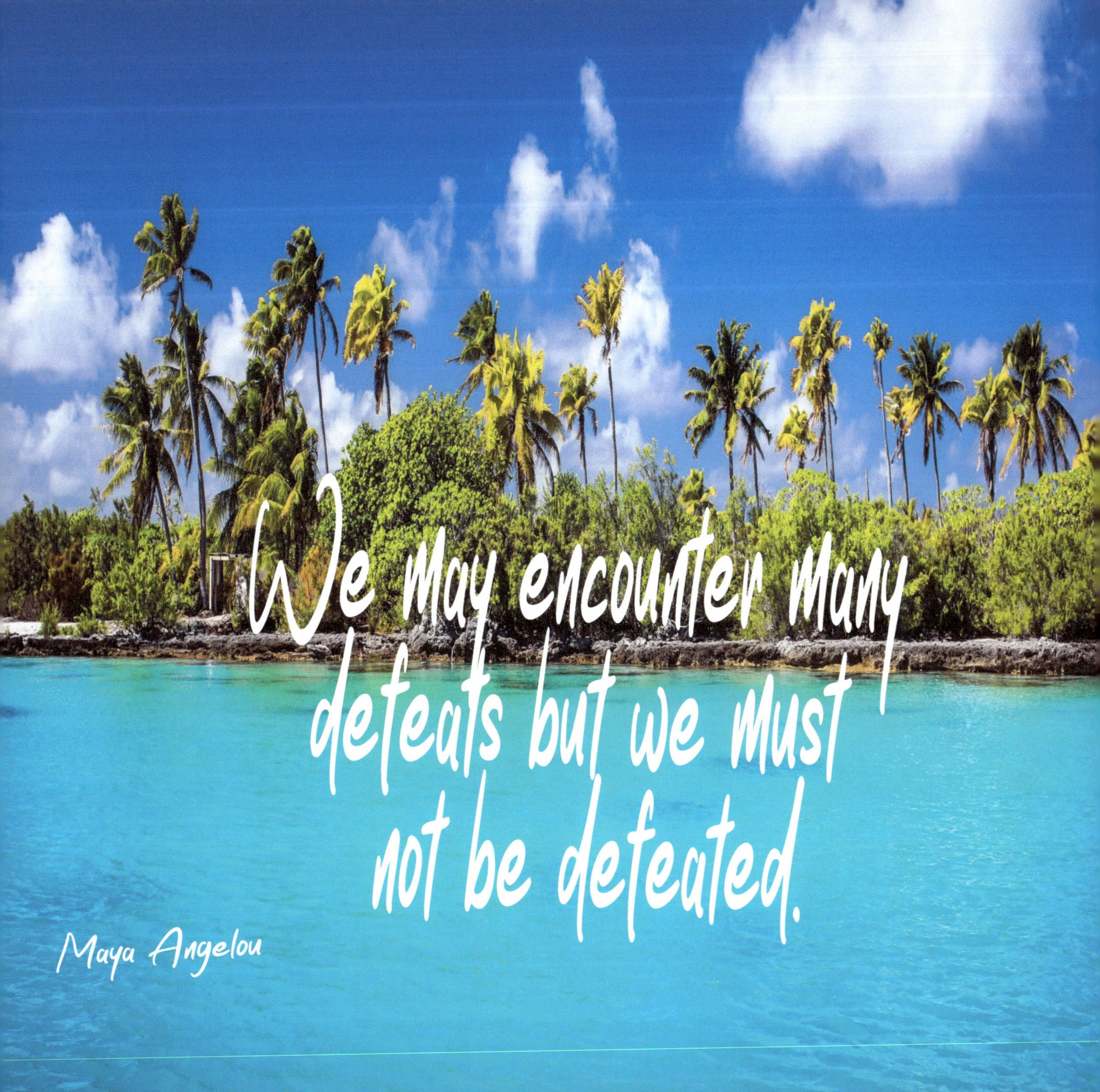

We may encounter many defeats but we must not be defeated.
Maya Angelou

JUL / 2021

S	M	T	W	T	F	S
				1	2	3
Independence Day 4	5	6	7	8	9	10
11	12	13	14	15	16	17
18	19	20	21	22	23	24
25	26	27	28	29	30	31

Entrepreneurs are great
at dealing with uncertainty
and also very good
at minimizing risk.

AUG / 2021

S	M	T	W	T	F	S
1	2	3	4	5	6	7
8	9	10	11	12	13	14
15	16	17	18	19	20	21
22	23	24	25	26	27	28
29	30	31				

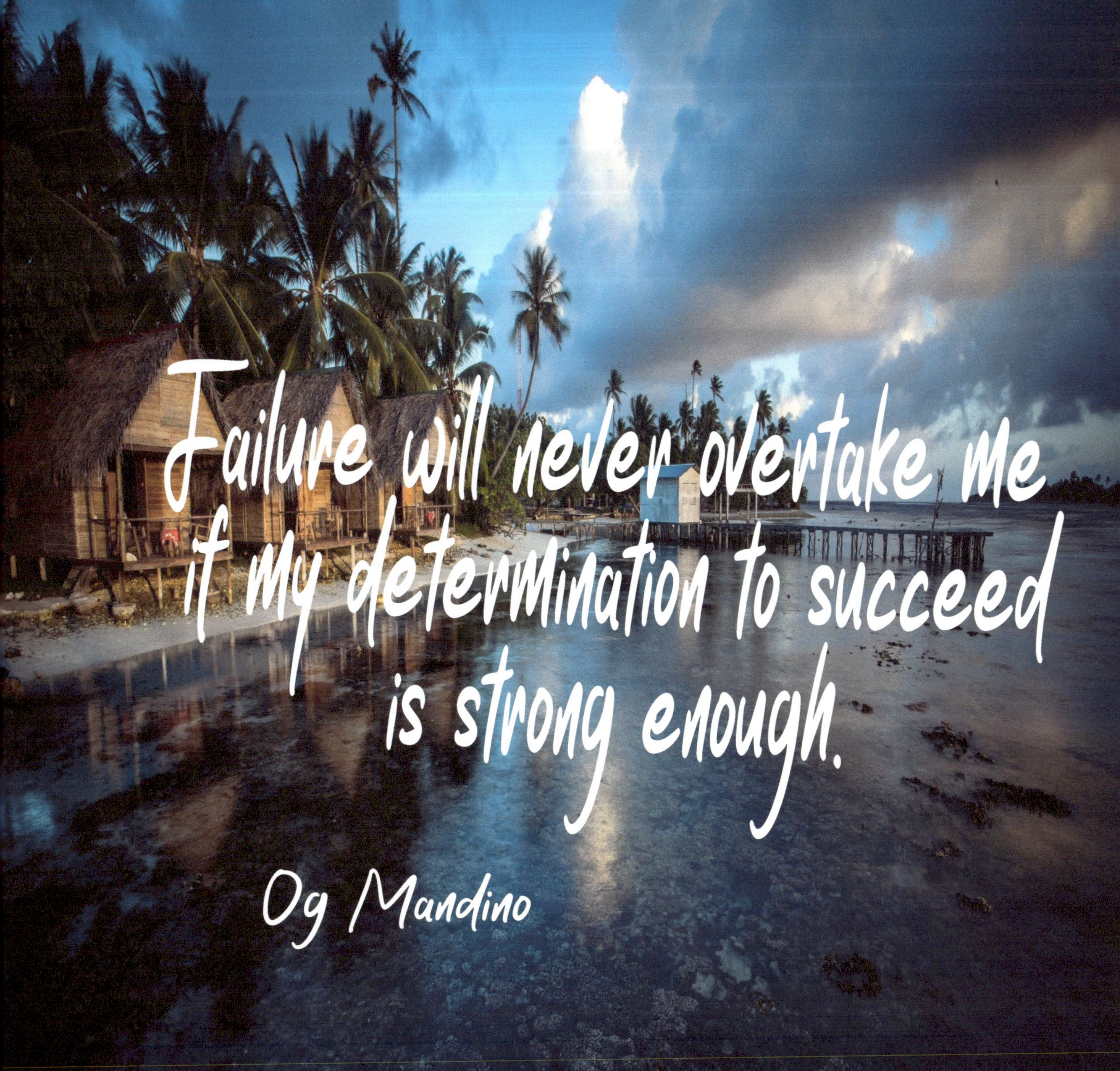
Failure will never overtake me
if my determination to succeed
is strong enough.

Og Mandino

SEP / 2021

S	M	T	W	T	F	S
			1	2	3	4
5	Labor Day 6	7	8	9	10	11
12	13	14	15	16	17	18
19	20	21	22	23	24	25
26	27	28	29	30		

Knowing is not enough; we must apply.
Wishing is not enough; we must do.

OCT / 2021

S M T W T F S
1 2
3 4 5 6 7 8 9
10 Columbus Day 11 12 13 14 15 16
17 18 19 20 21 22 23
24 25 26 27 28 29 30
31

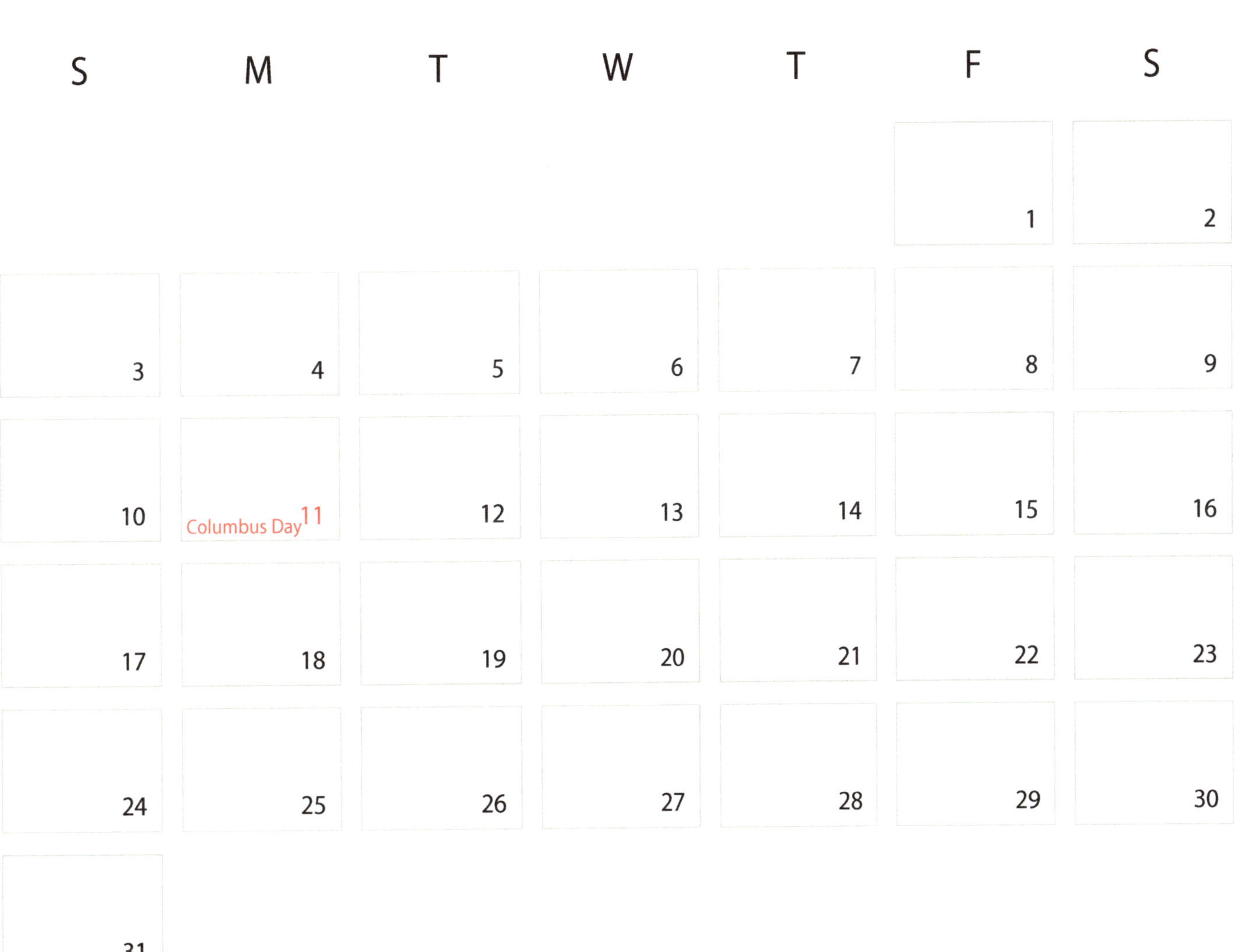

Imagine your life is perfect
in every respect:
what would it look like?

NOV / 2021

S	M	T	W	T	F	S
	1	2	3	4	5	6
7	8	9	10	Veterans Day 11	12	13
14	15	16	17	18	19	20
21	22	23	24	Thanksgiving 25	26	27
28	29	30				

We generate fears while we sit. We overcome them by action.

DEC / 2021

S M T W T F S
1 2 3 4
5 6 7 8 9 10 11
12 13 14 15 16 17 18
19 20 21 22 23 24 Christmas Day 25
26 27 28 29 30 New Year's Day 31

Whether you think you can
or think you can't,
you're right.

JAN / 2022

S
M
T
W
T
F
S
New Year's Day 1
2
3
4
5
6
7
8
9
10
11
12
13
14
15
16
17
Martin Luther King Jr
18
19
20
21
22
23
24
25
26
27
28
29
30
31

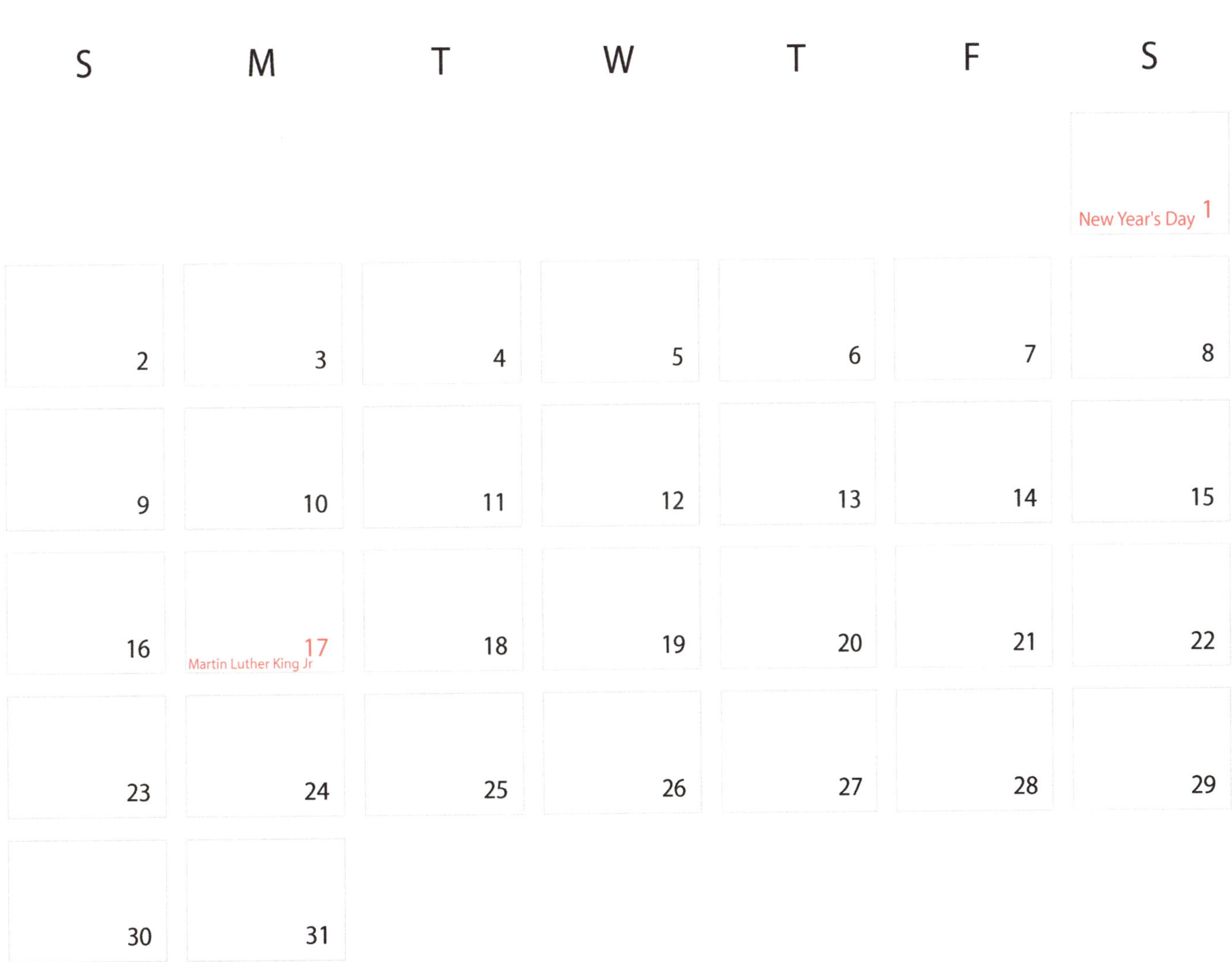

Security is mostly a superstition.
Life is either a daring
adventure or nothing.

FEB / 2022

S M T W T F S
1 2 3 4 5
6 7 8 9 10 11 12
13 14 15 16 17 18 19
20 Presidents' Day 21 22 23 24 25 26
27 28

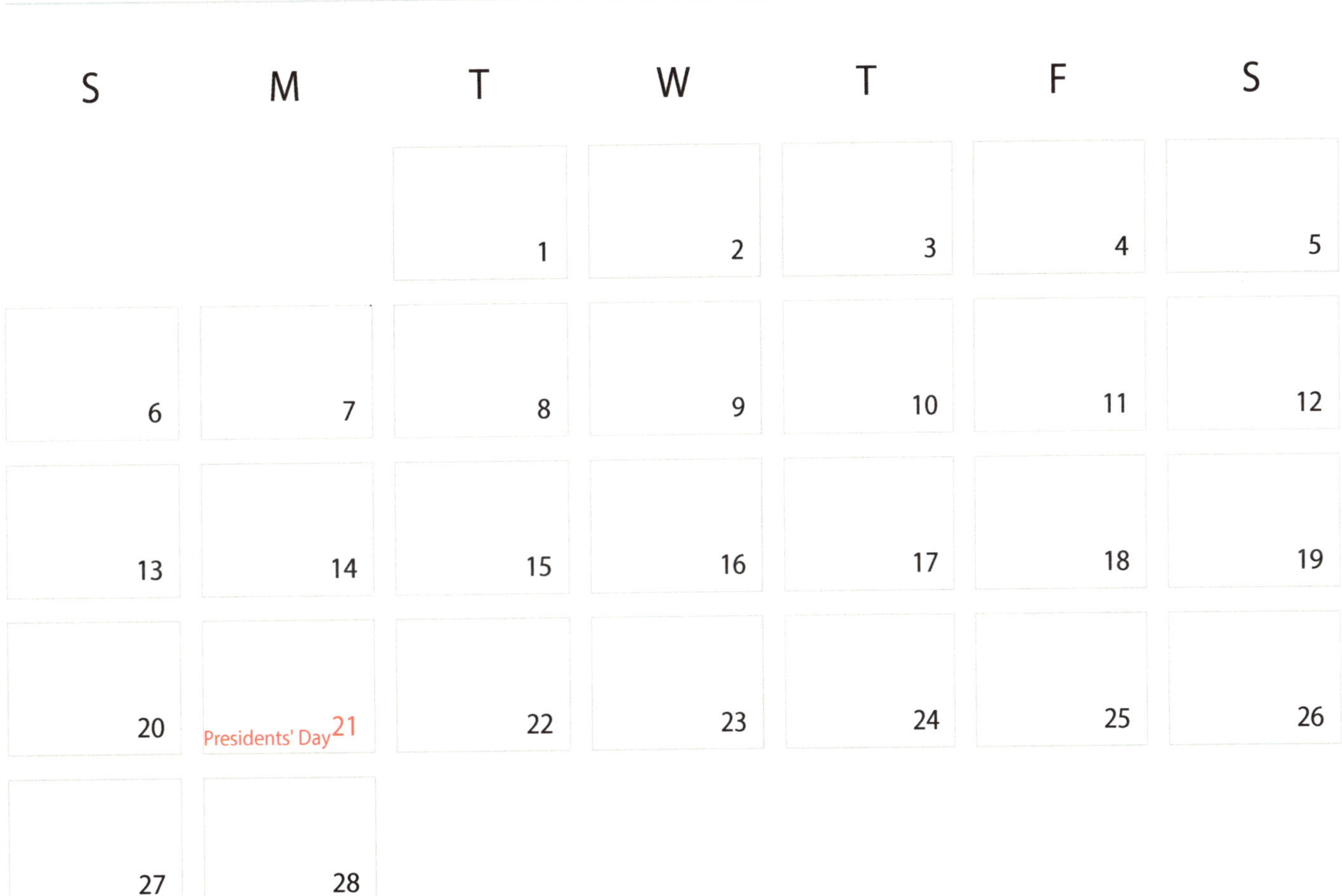

The man who has confidence
in himself gains
the confidence of others.

MAR / 2022

S	M	T	W	T	F	S
		1	2	3	4	5
6	7	8	9	10	11	12
13	14	15	16	17	18	19
20	21	22	23	24	25	26
27	28	29	30	31		

Creativity
is intelligence
having fun.

APR/ 2022

S	M	T	W	T	F	S
					1	2
3	4	5	6	7	8	9
10	11	12	13	14	15	16
17	18	19	20	21	22	23
24	25	26	27	28	29	30

The only limit to our realization
of tomorrow
will be our doubts of today.

Franklin D. Roosevelt